For Neal and [illegible]
All the best,
Richard
2019

# Mystic Pizzazz and Tiger Lilies

## Poems for the Spirit

**Richard Alan Bunch**

INFINITY PUBLISHING

ISBN 978-1-4958-1041-1



Published March 2016

INFINITY PUBLISHING
1094 New DeHaven Street, Suite 100
West Conshohocken, PA 19428-2713
Toll-free (877) BUY BOOK
Local Phone (610) 941-9999
Fax (610) 941-9959
Info@buybooksontheweb.com
www.buybooksontheweb.com

To the memory of my parents and sister

and to

Rita, Katharine, and Rick

*Ich lebe bei Tage*
*voll Glauben und Mut,*
*und sterbe die Nächte*
*in heiliger Glut.*

—Novalis, *Hymns to the Night*

(I live all day
Full of faith and courage
And die the nights
In holy fire)

Grateful acknowledgment is made to the following editors and publishers in whose publications (including online) earlier or final versions of some of these poems first appeared: *Northern Stars Magazine* and *In Dove Light.*

In addition, grateful acknowledgment is made to my wife, Rita, for her helpful support, suggestions and also pictures of the author in each of these volumes.

# Preface

Througout this work, from traditional to experimental, the reader will notice continuing experiments with language, voice, imagery, form, diction, rhythm, and so forth. Welcome to these language-experiments, my poems.

# Reflections for All Seasons

*All things share the same breath—the beast, the tree, the man—the air shares its spirit with all the life it supports.*

—Chief Osceola of the Seminole Native American tribe of Florida

*The Tao that can be spoken is not the eternal Tao.*

—Lao Tzu

*No man is an island entire of itself; every man is a piece of the continent, a part of the main... Any man's death diminishes me because I am involved in mankind and therefore never send to know for whom the bell tolls it tolls for thee.*

—John Donne, D.D.

*The more people I meet, the more I love my dog.*

—Mahatma Gandhi

*One day the absurdity of the almost universal human belief in the slavery of other animals will be palpable. We shall then have discovered our souls and become worthier of sharing this planet with them.*

—Martin Luther King Jr., Ph.D.

*In the flow of the holy spirit, one feels the divine life force coursing the pathways of existence, through all desires, all worlds, all thoughts, all nations, all creatures.*

—Kabbalah

*Cherish in yourself the birth of God.*

—Meister Eckhart, D.D.

*We need to find God, and he cannot be found in noise and restlessness. God is the friend of silence. See how nature – trees, flowers, grass- grows in silence; see the stars, the moon and the sun, how they move in silence...We need silence to be able to touch souls.*

—Mother Teresa

*With no bird singing the mountain is yet more still.*

—Zen Saying

*At the center of the universe dwells the Great Spirit. And that center is really everywhere. It is within each* of us.

—Black Elk of the Oglala Lakota branch of the Sioux nation

# Table of Contents

## Cunning Chromosomes

Needles of light descend the thundering
sea blue pillowy air
above well-pruned gardens
where it is time to plant
tears of ancestral remorse
as we finger rosaries
of cunning chromosomes.

A golden bough
hangs in the clearing
where prayers striate
the coastal hills
beneath the drip-sound of trees
like violins stirring notes with flutes.

We can hear the breathing
of runners
in the zest
of summertime joys
as unknown ships swan untold waves.

## Solitude

In this valley of a chosen fate,
trumpets of solitude troop forth
in heavily scented rooms
beneath stained-glass windows
with memories of pleasures long past.

A kiss of sea salt
touches our lips
as we pass fields

of standing corn, ancient woods,
and summer gardens
planted with zucchini,
tomatoes, and radishes.

We sit down to rest
in this solitude
where we are finally alone
with syllables
of unwounded vibrations.

Shifts of history,
powers that range above us,
feathers of sea birds,
and twists of wind in the treetops
parade by us
like coral faces
of waves on the banks of dawn.

## Tulum, Mexico

While sipping Corona and Heineken beers,
we look at our pictures
of the Mayan ruins in Tulum
as the waiter, Paulo,
brings us black jack fish, onions, and bread.

We are yet mesmerized
by the combination of clear water,
sea water below it,
and finally the river that flows
beneath the sea and is portrayed
as a channel used
by extraterrestrials to another world.

We can still feel
the cold sea coiled in our guts
and deep below
the soul-searching reefs

where we collected plankton
from outer space.

I remember how cold we were
not far from the *God of Winds Temple;*
how we welcomed the tropical sun!

As our shadows swooned on the sand,
the sea yet sings through my forehead.

## Will's Way

As his mistress murmurs and sings
a slumber dream of romance,
she continues painting
the spirit of the garden
in patches of color
with its hollyhocks, poppies, and sunflowers.

The air smells of thyme
since it is the time of flowering
in fields gone wild with cherry blossoms
beneath a sun that turns lunar
on moonlit oaks and hills.

Just after he realizes
there is a dark beauty at the core of light,
he inexplicably
embraces a bliss
when words fail
and manna
pours down like eloquent honey.

Sometimes that is just the way distance works
in beds of spring mountain leaves.

# Newborn Stars

"What ever you do,
stay wonderstruck in God," she said to us.

As young lovers,
we have almost nary a clue
as to what she meant.

You with your dark antiquity,
amber heart, coral lips,
and aloha shirt are what we know.

Yet her words engendered in us
a troubled sea of the mind
by unweeping trees
in our valley of newborn stars.

She also reminded us
to be friends with Buddha,
Moses, Jesus, and Mohammed.

Hard to be married to the divine
even in a community
lived in praise of the divine,
including intergalactic aliens.

So far, we have not
experienced divine madness
but only divine unforgetfulness,
especially in the splendor
of the hummingbird.

So pray for us sinners
as we age in love
until we rock
on the veranda
in our green treen chairs,
awaiting a revelatory vision
from a princely angel.

# Dana

As summer's
double bass twangs
atonally waft
into the beautiful,
we notice something
different about her.

She often refers
to why three poppies
may compose
the golden-red noise
of sunrise
and how her life's
canned copy
has taken flight
into spirit.

Here, along our
sea-washed coast,
where myrtle and ivy
stretch to the sea,
we talk with her
as we have quince
on brioche,
and red and yellow
Japanese plums.

She tells us how
she no longer plays
in a double bind
but has awakened
from the sleep of reality
to embrace
the magical element
in the iris of song.

Now she dances
on the navel of the earth

in a leaf-rich
crimson wind
where her third eye
and wisdom embrace.

## Turkish Coffee

As a copper headed waitress
at the *Calypso Horizons Café*
serves us Turkish coffee,
morning mists slowly
burn into day.

On this windless morning
a couple doze
between two willow trees.

Sunflowers, roses,
pansies and marigolds
paint a dramatic daybreak.

We also note a parrot's head
cocked to one side
then another
as lizards flicker
and dart into the lawn.

Despite all this,
we still feel
an unspeakable ache
how innocence vanishes in war.

In fact, innocence
sometimes occurs
between wars
in infant-birthing seas
even in lunges
of night beyond
the wrinkles of paradise

not just in the film
*Les Enfants du Paradis.*

War's shadow
on the wall
ever haunts
the heavenly bodies
in an attempt
to erase the third eye
in the middle of our foreheads.

## Gifts

In the seas of awareness,
some memories are negative,
especially the autos-da-fé
of those who thought
there are mulattos
and mestizos
that could match
Beethoven or Chopin.

But they could
as time's blood
flows through
saffron yellow summers
with a steely sense
of the unbelievable.

This all occurs in a state
with churches, temples,
many synagogues,
and strengths of vision
that include deer
roaming past
the edge of dreams,
and the first journey
of wild geese.

Mulattos and mestizos
cherish their
dyed in the wool talents,
gifts, and genius
since the divine
assumes the mark
of most desires
and gentle deeds of love.

## Rainbow Hearts

At passion's height
the lovers flee
into a wondrous evening twilight
which guides their way
through mystic mazes
and past
running blackberry vines.

They not only treasure
the soft animal
of their bodies
but the gift of fire
for lighting the way
past a golden storm of wheat
to new born seas
with their resurrection dolphins
and seafowl
squawking on deck
as the sea fishes
for heaven's boot.

They also celebrate
ancient dusky seas
in millions of waves
with their sea swells
in which ships, as now,
may founder and fall

in storm-riven seas
since violence empowers stress.

Yet her dovish spirit
comes to him
softer than a whisper
in a seashell.

They sense the
galaxy's journey is
not only silence
but string vibrations.

## Celestial Music

A player can strum strings
so far out
as to reach
the mouth
of a vaster music,
a spiritual closeness
beyond the speechless
blood of dreams
when your face
warms
with illuminations,
a sweetheart
in pomegranate flowers
swarming with new
memories
in the pearl glow of night.

You shift out
of the fire
into a new hymn
beyond yellowy weeds,
fig trees,
and a jungle grace
that smells beyond

the hissing foam
on sea-washed sepia beaches.

## Nights of Fools

Not just in earlier worlds,
but now as an hour
swims white with light
and even in kosher
weather fit for a king
with spit-blessed mountains,
it turns out men
can still be ambushed
by a woman who sleeps around,
a woman who vees her legs
in front of them,
who are vulnerable
to a dress drawn tight
across her ass.

Even national leaders,
CEOs, bankers, mafia men,
their muscled goons,
ministers, and
law enforcement folks,
often seen
in the catbird's seat,
are gudgeons
susceptible
to such skullduggery.

With cat's paws
on a lake or pond, the
moon slides pale
down the sky
even in a cloudscape
iridescent as a dream
on such nights of fools.

And to think
all these people,
unbeknownst to them,
are products
of a divine molding of
heaven with clay.

## Falling into Slumber

In thickets of truth,
we feel in time's womb,
the naked heat, hot as genesis,
of the peached suns of centuries.

Wind breathes green prairie waves
that sway bulrushes hiding moorhens
as gulls screech their souls.

As day enlightens into geometry,
we love by falling
into slumber with the sun.

Your delicate kisses
make noon purr in the grass.
We know in the hazards of
conversation
and earth-shifting debates
that every theology,
stammered in reflection,
ends as ideology
until we behold
the unveiled face of God.

## Hear the Chimes

Once you embrace
the sweet music
of the divine,

you can understand
the joys
of a tender
and liberated heart
as you walk along
a barrier beach
and hear the chimes
of heaven
in slow, lapping waves.

A raven of longing
perched on
a lovely evening's tree
is stitched
with ecstatic meditation,
awareness through prayer,
and breathing
the membrane
of primaeval silence.

These allow a glimpse
of infinite love
even in the petals
of pink carnations.

## Runes

With the mind wavering
with wishes and whispered voices,
every muscle
summons your intelligence
with nonfictions of the spirit
and stone runes
of chimeras
for on this sweet earth fountains
salt a glistening stillness.

We note sunlight in your hands
and as the river moves,
we smell the slur of the sea.

Soon the eggshell of dark
will begin to climb the copper hills.

## Dark Fragrances

Amid wild connections,
including laughing eunuchs
we find in this dusky summer
topped by scrawny masts
and dark fragrances of dreams
on nights too turbulent
for sleeping,
our hearts
are still drawn to the Milky Way.

Healing eyes and the soft breezes of God
rock us to sleep
in the peace of sycamores
and mindscapes
deep in clover and grass.

Meanwhile, spinach, corn, and carrots
continue their
flowery bursts like irises and calypsos.

## Bumper Stickers

As we stroll along
in the shade cast by elms and pines
and the shifting scent
of jasmine and orchids,
we note bumper stickers
that trumpet a new theology,
one with hermetic pentameters.

Mutating hues vibrate
a new geography of green isles,
purple coves, and speeding waves.

With love's labor,
you say what you say
because it is poetry
in the circumference
of presence of muses
beneath those amber
lean-tos and rerun dreams.

## Yoshi

He is a meditator
in the moon-forming night
who often engages in
seemingly endless reflection
as he sits among wild plums
and blood-purpled pomegranate seeds.

At times he asks
"my God why do you not exist?"

He is not some wild
and primitive man like Enkidu.
He knows the divine
can work miracles.

Sometimes he sits for so long
he cannot feel his legs
and then out of the blue
he sings a song for nobody
in minor broken chords.

A cicada pauses to listen to his song.
In spite of his doubts,
his sense of grace remains unshaken.

# Turquoise Rain

On a spiritual night
after a turquoise rain
there sighs whispers
of morning prayers.

In the ghostly words of faith,
we sense each incarnation
takes faith
even for hundreds of riders
from states of sorrow
since longing often shapes a life.

As a tangerine sun
splits the mountain,
we remark a leafy footbridge
leading to acres of blue-violet grapes
and the quiet kiss of flowers
as a heron lifts from the fir tree.

Signs from falling stars
glimmer as we end the day
rowing our skiff on an evening pond.

# Satanic

In this tribe,
Old Nick is the low man
who swims in twilight
among sleeping swans.

Autumn, you observe,
comes slowly this year,
trickling like pitch from a prune tree.

We knock on wood.

Heat of the sand feels good
after a cold swim
under a noontide sun.

He prefers hedonism
and feigns a mute respect
for nirvana and poets
who cleave the earth
with their truths.

He declines to wear
a Hopi bracelet or
listen to the
Navajo Night Chant.

Through a moonlit cedar
emerge silver apples
and silky sky
beneath a caravan of stars.

We barely discern
the playbook of his lady loves
and ghosts after we're gone.

## Notes for a Future

Beneath a sinking sun
in a summer of enduring visions,
we discover music
sets up a ladder
to our moon-flanked
futuristic Y's
amid a cloud of stars.

Along the seaboard,
there are oceanic secrets
among the driftwood, sea irises,
ice plants, and seaweed.

We also note mandarin ducks
floating side by side
as a heron glides overhead.

The seacoast cries out
for the spirit
as well as white petals
on the water as we feel
the powerful pull of time's tides,
those eyes that speak to us
like sacred conch shells.

## Lorelei

While listening
to the cicada in the fig tree,
she recalls dreamy memories
of the horses of summers past
in fields where tulips fade.

And now feasts her eyes
on that primitive fury
of sun-struck tides
where silent ships
between dark and dawn
plod across the sea.

As she listens to the miracle
of ascending measures
in the shadows of
St. Teresa Benedicta
of the Cross steeple,
she also cherishes
the country churchyard
with a slush of self-healing feeling.

# Yeasty Drifts

Sometimes it is not
a matter
of ocular dominance
but a symphonic poem
just to behold
and drink with both eyes
how marsh marigolds
color the meadows
in yeasty drifts
beneath a heaven
that childs us
with words and roots
as the sun slants
through the madroñas and pines.

While coyotes often howl
in the mountains behind us,
our farm is
near the salmon sea
with its churning tides
and star-like seagulls
that soar and glide.

By mid-afternoon,
the sea's skin shines
with roving masts
and dyed canvases
as kestrels hover
and swallows shoot overhead.

That star,
our lemon yellow sun,
is also mistress
of greening forests
and passionflowers.

# Sunrise Sabbath

*for Rita*

As I taste the sacrament
of sun and female sea,
windjammers and their crews,
I continue to witness
your image in the tide.

With its lapping waves
thundering from the deep,
the sea sings like shells
among the untitled and oversexed.

The splendor of your hazel eyes
excites me even now
since I could not,
altered in the cornea's slant,
love any other woman.

I observe mandarin ducks
floating side by side
as I taste a Santa Rosa plum
while sipping a Trappist beer
at the See of Bees café.

Some say dreams
are one way
to a terra incognita
yet there are handfuls of stars,
madness, and white flame moons
in a house of dreams.

Yet in my dreams,
I behold you on an antique clock
dressed like a Sabbath at sunrise.

# Blue Heaven

Our goal is to keep alive
our recollection of her courage
when empathy
replaced her heart of stone
by rewriting lives
in her dust
as in the time present
when swallows convene
in the treetops
and summer still smolders
in the hinterlands.

She would bring us warm bread,
olives, and red wine.

We pooh-poohed those
who did not cotton to her
as they drank from
their daily cups of innuendo.

But, for us, she was sweetness
in the air after a summer storm,
an eclipse of a sun burned orange,
and our daily prayer giving of thanks
as we drank holy water
from the globe of genesis.

# Dancing Folks

In spite of this stubbornly
closed world
where seeing is often deceiving
and death is a long voyage,
I dance and dance amid the miracles,
including your voice
of vibrant light

and liberating laugh
surrounded by
the graveyard howl
of your infinity.

As I compose this
invisible poem
beneath a rainbow's perfume,
and in dream after lovely dream,
we only know that what lasts
can bring us to a truth
such as this our visible world
is composed of
what we don't know
about the divine.

## Sacré Coeur

As I come into this solitude
and wave to the shore
where vines and bay leaves
embrace and
in the light of sun and moon,
I realize that by God
as salt in water
or a sunbeam reflected
in a pewter dish in Göerlitz,
I live as Christ
broods in all features
such as the skin
over an atrium afternoon.

You and I
may marry at Sacré Coeur
and maybe help
shape the human race
into fragrances of love
among the living.

As the water rises,
I soon notice my pole
a long way down the river.

## Tinkle Tinkle

In the realm of the flesh,
there abide lips of rising blood,
digital bandits with warheads,
the tinkle tinkle of violin strings,
dancers in the dance of the dead,
white smoke of incense,
mandarin voices,
cows with cuds of wine,
milky valleys of light,
Angus bulls in a field
the color of summer blood
as well as crew cuts and afros
of the maze.

Meanwhile, by the labial heart
of this summer willow,
I sip my Evian water,
nibble on jack cheese
with mushrooms,
and ponder sweet-scented
irises and orchids.

## Voyaging

Voyaging clockwise
between shadow and splendor,
one of the mountains
touches me deeply
as I notice aging lines
that sleep on the stones
near candlewood trees
growing not that far from a woodland's face.

When it comes to pursuing
the fate of everything,
sometimes there are
mystical disclosures
when it comes to honeyeaters,
purple finches, western tanagers,
and Bonaparte's gulls.

Meanwhile I sip my
sweet, hot, and blond coffee,
eat popcorn and rice cakes,
and study the heart-shaped head
of a rock above
an undrubbed seaboard with erotic sand.

## Sitala

As we stroll the dunes,
we mark a straggle of gulls
and the lack of quiet in their eyes.

With binoculars we can see
in the day's dazzle
the shoreline of that
island of eggs
with its green scent of flowers
and where we met Sitala,
a spirit who can walk
with a serpent upon the sky
and cherishes swallows
that fly over fields of mustard.

We know electricity rules
our life
but she taught us
the beauty of a black confetti
of crows and,
as blue mountain winds sigh,

songs of the fluent elk,
pheasant, and eagle.

## Divine Theater

Long before we could try
our lines off stage
have visions or paint dreams,
we were amino acids,
crawling glaciers,
enchanted pillars of fire,
or confederate ghosts
of black Scots
who clashed at the Roman wall
in a spicy wind of sky,
and spun tales, myths and metaphors.

Even in a mediaeval lake,
we knew
a galaxy shone
in the shoe-button
eyes of a trout.

We learned to harvest
ears of corn,
hunt prey as well as each other,
laid out almonds in the sun,
prayed to the sun god,
delighted in bodies of water,
and after a storm
picked among
the debris of trees
many coming horizons.

# Conjunctions

1.

The rabbit's fur drips with rain
beneath the redwoods. In the wood
summer still sleeps.

2.

The sage muses
on the meaning of being
and its disclosive art:
a novel language for the dying.

3.

In a subway station down the eye of a pistol
aging is kinder than winter
contained by the savage heart.

4.

Pearls lying in darker waters
secrete ambition, the prize of
knives. They pry into secret lives.

5.

Canopy of the galaxy, the body's sacred time,
an explosion to lift the blessed,
for all spiritual destinies
in matter begin.

6.

Worms crawl out of apple-dreams
and go back to those unheard refrains,
lineals of the ancestral blood.

7.

Viruses appear at prime time,
once more fusing body with mind,
coiling around our comedy
with the bronze of winter.

8.

Serpents of death
squirm through membranes,
anonymous, double-minded,
shuffling with the odds. They too
enliven biographies of grenadine
amid the driftwood decor.

9.

Heart of sky, heart of earth,
parents of return,
all-too-soon recast
the violin's sound and its tenor,
idioms that implicitly disclose
the spectrum of silence.

## Blue of the Blue

In the shade
of summer treetops
and amid the ritual
anthem of blackberry wine,
blue of the blue vervains,
breadths of the starry savannahs,
we learned
to cultivate a habit
cradled between a sorrel fox
and an eggshell hare
regarding earth-created
equations measuring the horizon.

It expands the caucus
of mandarin poppies
and orchid asters.

In the scent of prayer,
the flickers of perhaps,
the sun flowered
kingdom of promise,
and amid the onion domes
of orthodox churches,
we learned to forge death
from life
to a life
beyond the earthly beyond.

## The Sexton

As moonlight bounds
softly forth on the grass,
it's benedictine pallor
falls into his eyes,
enfleshing his dream
of the beautiful,
and casts
snake-plant shadows
onto shell game shells
and their roses of Jericho.

As his wife, Geneviève,
cooks beef stew with garlic,
they discuss
why two beached boats
languish on the edge
of the berm
and one rests
among the reeds.

As Norway maple leaves
wink and silver panther-shaped

cloudlets float by,
he tells her
he wants a salad for breakfast
since he will help tomorrow
with a funeral of grave language.

While he does all that,
she will be fixing their computer.

When he comes home,
they can sip green tea
and work again
on the sleepwalkers
in their family tree.

## By Chance

In this world where everything
is chance whether it is playing poker,
real estate, banking, making war,
committing murder
and taking revenge,
you have, for instance,
to learn to cut
the thread of revenge
lest a snake
make a nest in your skull.

No, for the sake of honor,
courage, and self-respect
you can, with the passion of summer,
lean toward the light of paradise
in the city of the sun.

That way, you can act well
your part and cultivate creativity
and make, for example,
bohemian sacred art
with its lapis lazuli lakes of sky

and sacred songs
inspired by crystal vases,
make it your lifestyle
to do no harm
so that it zigzags its way
through the house
in the fellow-feeling
of the forest and the sea, or
mapping many passageways
to the caring human heart.

## New Arrivals

When you arrive,
arrive with affection
and new sounds.

One word of Danish
has changed the whole town.

Outside the window
filled with lemon trees,
you can hear
the rustle
of lilacs and carnations
in our hexagon-shaped garden,
and watch the graceful ibis
and several mallards
in the lagoon.

That is one way
to keep your mind tender
and your nerve-endings simpatico.

And then there is love
that shakes with hopes,
lies, the past of futures,
curls of lips,
and sometimes lethal entanglements.

Keep perspective
and you can avoid
bad seasons for sale.

What you want to do
is end up in the horizons
and maybe, just maybe,
you can envision
the dark face of God.

## Starry Nights from Afar

You will be all right long after I am
gone since the stars shone from afar
long before we arrived here, a shadow
of us, a billion stars, will remain
as far as nonsense may
be.

Remember, as you walk through
the shamrock fields of God
and glimpse
shocking coral of the afterlife
with its rainbow songs and laughter,
that darkness, all the way
to dream's distant music,
is only night
to eyes that look for it.

## Time's Weather

We are always travelers
sometimes living on nothing
in a foreign land
where mist rises
from the valleys
and where we can hear

trees grow
with those listening hands.

Here we are born alive
and the divine
with a dormant gene
blossoms in subtle shifts of light.

We realize love is more than this place
where we have visions
of unbleached sails,
snail shells pooled
with time's weather,
the reappearance of minor chords,
and ancestral features in embryos.

## What is Given

We know what is given
can be taken away.

As the sun dates the earth
and a church spire juts
into a sky that suggests
expanding star charts
as the spiritual in the making
that paradise
is the eternal now.

Then we can lounge
among rose petals
and listen as love and tenderness
make one swish
like a flute
whose sound echoes itself.

In the lexicon
of devotion's detail,
it is an image

that cannot be escaped
until it is painted.

## Upper Room

In the psyche's upper room,
a confession slowly unwinds
as the wind stirs the willows.

As I wait for the sky of sun,
the legendizing
of the sea's erotic waves,
and winter lilacs,
I realize the clock cannot
with one invisible hand
hold back the old fathers
that go on to the hereafter.

As I consider this vision,
I finish my succotash and potatoes
beneath peach leaves
next to a stone wall.

The upper room
is a persistent melody
that uplifts and dreams.

## My Mystic Rose

When I say this, I am not saying this
in jest as some mythological
golden age poet
but sometimes out of the burned-out,
tangled heap of felled wartime bodies
death makes a gift of life.

Though your mother
died in giving birth to you,

the handful of earth
you are
with your red rose-bordered hems,
urges me to lift up my eyes
to the stars and give thanks.

You are my mystic rose
with spiritual wisdom
and knowledge
in a galaxy of old times
swirling in jazz and honeysuckle
beneath the sun's silky leaves.

## Horoscope

You check your horoscope:
"Neptune sliding out of *Pisces*
takes your delusions
of forgetfulness with it."

Most around us
hear your raffish laughter
in this cornflower blue summer.

You love bonfires
at the beach
as tour buses line
the resort parking lot.

As your fictive kin,
I am part of your family
of different ages
counting up
whether it is among
the electric hums of crickets,
caverns in a mountain side
dotted with susurrant oaks,
or beneath flights

of migrating cranes
and monarch butterflies.

We know art,
even as a mirage,
defies brevity
in a stelliferous sky
or green isles
bunched with lilies
glorious as Solomon
silent among old stones
warmed by the western sun.

Such are some sacramental visions
of a wide-arched grace.

## Summer Angels

A spirit army of summer angels
is approaching
from every quarter
of interstellar space.

They have no need
for Hero of Alexandria's
holy water dispenser.

It is a mid-winter summer,
a summer before summer.

They inspire me
to hum a daydream
among the flowers,
sing hymns
to the marshes and foothills,
spin black silk times into fish,
discover as doctors of energy
undoctored dreams
in my looking glass

as starlight wavers
and moon shadows
merge with darkness.

The stage is now set
for the eternal now.

## Psyche

With quite a bit of oomph
she is the earthquake of her town.

As rice cooks and apples
are stewed into apple butter
for our rolls,
I ponder how she walks
on half of the sky.

She often takes walks
beneath clouds of crimson
and flamingo
or a full moon
sullied with a purple haze.

She adores art such as
Michelangelo's *Dying Slave,*
automatic writing,
the precision of engraving,
the whims of drawing,
and Barber's *Dover Beach.*

She prizes ships,
even those without a sail,
works on her own boat
with a yellow hammer
that is as light as a feather.

She brings a kind of gladness,
beatific light with her every step
and a heart veined with compassion.

## Desert Night

An infinite desert,
the other face of night
in the darkest light
summer's tropical waters
by winter's wind that
proffers itself to the earth.

We are everlasting travelers
as I lie with you
and you with me
from our love of the blue beyond
to the auroral oak pews
and red altar carpet.

We sense beauty is a relation
between rainbows,
the ascending sun,
scarlet blossoms,
and that eyelash of morning,
the dawn.

Where the word moves,
the sea moves. We go on living.
We let the living discover
a poetic wisdom dwells in the desert.

## Fertility

When it comes to
the fertility of water,
steel blue tides show a power
to break even windbreaks

in a feverish
sea-driven fog
as sons of a sunflower moon.

For hunters of the spirit,
day is wreathed
in the starlight of the body.

Sometimes silent lips
speak of a sunlit wilderness
where there is time
to think about life,
about poets
such as Voznesensky
or arsonists like Nero.

To be sure, not all losses
attributable to wind,
water, or humanity
may ever be restored.

## The River of Mindfulness

As history plods
among ancient faces
and earth's pucker of promise,
despite the thrash
of human presence
with its bruised peaches,
everywhere,
including the Great Spirit's realm,
is the book I love
with its summers of dream.

As I pull lotus blossoms
and maple leaves
out of the pool,
I celebrate how imagination
dances along the river

of mindfulness
with its rocks and sandbars,
beneath a hunting moon
and sea-broad sun.

Sometimes imagination
is the negative of day,
a perpetual twilight,
in a region of the drowned.
Fortunately, I also understand
that in the sound of oars
and record of waves,
silence also resides beyond time
in a beatific mansion.

## Sister Sheena

As you read my palm
at the *Bloodlines Café*,
you notice
how my lifeline includes
a movement
toward infinite chances
of the barely possible
through which we may
shape ourselves.

You point out
how our senses
include not only
the unfathoming depths
of sleep, but the
long shadows of
light-conferring desire,
how we are made
from words
amid landscapes
of voices
encircled by

pulsating fireflies
mirrored in water,
dusky trees
that chat with the wind,
midnights
of philosophy
beneath dewfall stars
as the hours slip by
in summer robes.

## Irish Blessing

Sipping a brew at the westernmost
pub in Galway, a priest
of the muses describes
how to get past counting
railroad ties
and points to boats
in full sail
on a wind-swept sea.

Meanwhile by a pond
lovers watch diving ducks
such as the scaup and
redheaded pochard.

She is not the first
to be dazzled
by a lover's wavy hair
and his eyes blue as the ocean.

Next to them
is a strobe-lit garden
of sunlight with
roses of Jericho and daffodils.

They appear to have
a strong faith
that fevers the blood

and will withstand the assaults
of tragedy through the years.

As they crawl into bed,
music on their travels
will nourish
their fondest memories.

## Caleb and Carondelet

On a deep sapphire day
as the sun glimmers
and glows,
many are the human arts,
including fantastic lovers
who espouse each caress
beneath mansard roofs,
hum the chimes of Paris,
and cherish
the Spanish lace
she makes.

He designs fountains
once only dreamed of
and chairs studded with rubies.

She knows each dream
may be a creative rerun
with its own sweet dangers.

Whether on an island
where tides etch
their eelgrass rhythms
or the mainland
where fields
can lure us afar,
only what lasts
can bring us
new theologies

and arrangements
of daisies and passionflowers.

## Journey's End

No longer asleep
in your prodigious soul's
summer, fall, winter, spring,
the dialect of the tribe
eats up darkness
as time's body
drives us to a point
that is our journey's end
of memory and mourning.

Like a half-crazed wheel,
her heart still craves him
even while shaking roots
divine and deep
in a solitude
where all waters meet
a bullying wind
off breaking waves
near a pigeon loft
tickled pink with whispers
and marine shadows.

Such is the persistence
of craving.

## Heat

Purgatorial fires
and unchecked desires
saunter in small country churches
beneath a desert sun
as we stare into

our blistering valley
between gigantic saguaros
and speeding semis on the highway.

So refreshing it is
to dive in from our catamaran
and take a swim
among those who want liquor,
laughter, and women.

As night approaches,
it finally starts
to cool down
in the moonlight
and shifting columns
of starlight.

We nurse our sparkling water
as we finish
our fish tacos and beef enchiladas.

## Unicorn Magic

As we enjoy beer and potato bread
at the Jacaranda Café
and strong sunlight
at the height of summer,
I ponder the idea
that we are more
than violence
and cunning
with gunmetal gray eyes.

Maybe somewhere
in the brain's memory
is a long-forgotten story
that in the furthest
reaches of dead time
unicorn magic

animates
the beginnings of life
from protozoa
to chest-high ferns
and woods full
of wild garlic
and orangutans.

Like angels in the morning,
wave music flows
time after times
toward seaboard sands.

Now can we see
how poets in love
resonate with
melodious strains
and an inborn tenderness.

## Eryn

She is the loveliest
and most learned of angels
even when the sky darkens
with Canada geese migrations
and the sea shouts and hisses
toward a lost gold
and lingering green future,
not to mention
those lightning-flashed moments
of the Pacific.

She is a synthesis
between hibiscus
and the yellow disks of sunflowers.

I love to sleep
in the light of her shadow

for she quickens
the beats of my heart.

That's the way it has been
since the first chaos of things.

## Whispers Throb

In the moral mindscape
of a primaeval forest,
a land of promise,
where whispers throb
with vision and desire
in the old tongue,
there occurs
a sea-green vision
of a sacramental earth.

In the refracted light
of a unforgiving summer sun,
there are
dawnlit roots
smelling of rosemary
or on the beach
where a godlike sheen emerges
as unconscious waves replace
the fealty of memory,
flowers, with their susurration leaves,
bloom in their own time
as a cargo of diamonds
arrives at a navy dockyard.

## Sorcha

As a theologian, Sorcha
ponders eschatology,
another scheme of time,
as a solution

for the lunatic binge
who spend their time
keeping up with the goats,
(not to mention the Joneses)
on a jumping bed
in unearthing
ancient astronauts
and comparing today's flesh
sown with instincts and salt.

In the warm fragrances of summer,
she understands,
even in unfurnished concepts,
the swoop of making a kindness
of necessity
in these sun-blanched villages
set against deep green forests
where the sharp-sighted lynx dwells.

As the sea begins again and again,
she enjoys dolphins diving
through each drop of surf
full of squalls.

## Erin go bragh

We spend our day
English sunbathing
in unerring solar beams
and futzing around
at a partially sunken coast.

Southward we note
how reefs
divide newborn
and inland seas.

Cliffs that include
granite and greywacke

map our delight
during our biblical
feast of days
when we breathe
traditional for the infinite.

Through the thickets
of time,
we see roses of Jericho
that blossom
in and out of season.

Tomorrow night is
the Erin go bragh-themed dance.

As our hearts
are in melodious harmony,
we plan to wear shamrock
leprechaun hats and sweaters.

This night,
as we leave the beach
for the Kingfisher Café,
the moon rises
amid a crowd of stars
and we soon mark
the constellation, Orion's belt.

# Crumbs of Clouds

As we dine
on cottage pie
and frankfurters
at the Rio Nido Café,
we note a brook
puckered with liquid light
dressed in splendor
and listen

to the bubbling foam
of a restive sky blue sea.

In a place
peopled with sins,
we also know it to be
a place where
genuine mystics
are gathering
for these souls' wedding
before they honeymoon
with caresses
on the streams of skin
in a chariot
of the gods.

As fireflies light up
the night,
her eyes rise
in his dreams,
his songs
are filled with lips,
and with one touch
of God's robe,
they are seduced
into humbly honoring
themselves with
whole nights and days
in their lovesome veins.

They know the difference
between accident
and essence
beneath crumbs
of clouds and kisses
in the living night.

# Zen Sight

1.

To be the sound of water
is to be between
the sound of white
and whitewater.
No longer to need
to rhapsodize or canonize
the eschatology
of summer trees.

2.

A certain joy shapes
our loneliness
and finally fashions it.
A gateless gate: here
your thinkings crystalize.

3.

Rain beating down on the rain
on an old man in Tennessee;
a parrot cocks her head,
the river keeps flowing.
They all listen
as stars in the fall
fall asleep.

4.

A new way to spoon
eaten thoughts
into a pregnant emptiness:
here, step into this
picture of four pears
on top of a blue mountain,

yes, the one there with
a blue wren on a blue branch.

5.

The work of breeding dreams:
the circular skins of me
and me. How final, how free
the wild swans
in a bleeding twig's kingdom.

6.

By plum trees
the lovers lying there. And the moon partly
hidden. All together their
lines, which you can barely
make out, map out a sacred space;
centered thus, they all share
the waterfall at dusk.

7.

Nothing exists. Here hangs
a metaphysical tale
on comedians in the dark.
Striking a blue match,
the muscular one plays
a mean jazz guitar
with a clear blue voice
of a sound clearing.

8.

Upon a sun-hammered hill
clusters of knotted oak
paint the true body.
Like trusted habits
shedding snakeskin,
the fallen leaf's

eternity
resexualizes.

9.

Amid parabolas
of soul
and skeins of memory,
a squirrel sits
motionless
as we pass.
Deepening, the river
swirls once again.

10.

As stars skate
across the pond,
a marigold motions
with this aside:
*travel light,* she says,
*if you wish to approach*
*the fathomless plum.*

11.

Answer to the riddle
of April rain:
brazened hawks encircle
yellowing flesh
made of yellowing flesh
made of the music of more.

## Testament

In the corridors
of a blooming spring
with corn growing waist-high
and resurrections all around,

we may look with love
at love
for there is a sweet
sacred line in loving.

In the ancestral
family of things,
lions of passion, white fire,
and wild honey
have the scent
of dreams that do not lie
just as writing
of the sea
can be etched
in each swell.

And this is so
even when last roses
open their last wills
of freedom
beneath a sky
flushed pink
when the moon is red.

## Between Parentheses

As we eat tuna fish sandwiches,
God, like all desire,
appears holy
at our window
with skylarks that skylark
above fields
with hidden lizards and king snakes
(the heart at times craves façades).

While we sample the catches
of years and
to those drums of sunlight,
the morning spreads

over the beaches
like spattered sand
and finds kinship with
fingers of water.

In a bed of wind we lounge.
There, we often sense
stars blink deep thoughts
as forenoons
and high noons come and go.

There, we may also
make a toast to our dreams
in a dream catcher
and meet makers
of new spiritual forms
and technologies.

## Secrets

Your welcome music,
an oasis shaded with burning palms,
delights the fall of your clear-voiced,
wind-tossed waters
next to fields of blood-red poppies
among neighboring hills
and dreaming forests
of lazy maples and Douglas fir.

Beneath an albino moonlight,
circuits of bare desire
hide caves of religious ritual
just as the voiceless Sphinx
seems to paw a secret power
of electrical blue.

In this silent shade of blue,
our secret comes closer in the light.

# Innocent Color

"Is this real,
the life I am living?"

I'm always
asking about a time
when time
can be banished
as I sip Courvoisier cognac
with my evening coffee.

Each day
tracks of my hunger
stalk through acres
and acres of jack pine,
the hard music
of stonecutters,
and killdeer,
one of the voices
off the river banks,
and slapping waves
on the seaboard.

As the earth keeps breathing,
a kingfisher dips
and rises over the marsh.

Once the lemon sun
drops into sunset,
fog takes dominion everywhere
and drifts after me
into the spirit land
where color colors innocent.

# The Birth and Death of Venus

## I. Symbols

I have this heart for you
In sea time upon the face of the Nile.
A need in pictures thought in abstraction:
Yes, this heart is a painter's dream, of nothing
On top of nothing, on top of nothing
Still a picture, a painting.
See these strokes: how bold about the eyes,
Pictures snow birds singing with their red feathers.
But the pictures are still here.
Give me your ears, o bards of Avon!
And those frescoes of bearded smiling anguish
Upon my auricle.
Paint them not on top of nothing.
Is this Ilium?[1]
No, not at all, sir.
Burning?
Yes within Agamemnon.[2]
What canvas is this, o human heart?
Have you altered this distracted musing?
Take away those symbols that do clang
In my ears and pierce the senseless everyday
On top of nothing but emptiness, emptiness.
Poets' words die in a breath of eternity,
they dwell in higher realms of senselessness.
Then kiss time goodbye for sorrow will preserve
The profile for eternity's babbling idiocy into
Which the artist rests. Momentary madness called love
By you is worth an eternal second.
But these fragments are spent in time's
Full emptiness.

Selah

---

1 Ilium: ancient city in Asia Minor that was site of the Trojan War.

2 Agamemnon: Greek commander in Trojan War.

# II. Words

What do you say, old man? In London town?
He spoke with a chin of age:
Who but we fools could endure
The wretched beat of humankind?
Belief's persecution, love's mirage,
The uncertain certainty of death
And wonder of the human brain?
The choice tray of good and evil?
And life's sweet sad tale?
No, old man, do not mock me with insolence.
This canvas is timeless,
This heart beats out more tympanic rhythms
That puts fear into the gods.
Speak! Speak! And let us hear your words!
We are as fools!
And time, the world's pulse
Shall hang itself and dissolve into a fathomless grave,
Ceasing on a wing spread,
Only to contract itself into immortal ashes
Beneath an azure heaven.
Again you mock me. Have you not the problem?
You must obey obey obey these impulses?
You too are a school lad who grows into understanding.
Never trust love's promising whispers.
Again you mock me old man!
Could it be that you, you are too blind to see?
I shall mark you for my own inglorious tale.
You shall never reject this canvas, its warmth as rare
In the fields green and growing wild in the sun's flowers;
Mortals feel, I tell you
Mortals feel
Mortals…
Yes, when young they do!
The poor helpless ones!
They cannot help their passion
For it is bold and a fantasy and pants
In its thirst for forbiddenness.

Ha! This is a merry lark! You don't know what you say or do.
How do you know this picture cannot engulf you?
I am desireless.
But it shall make you again pregnant.
My age is past the days when the blood swells with desire.
But what about it?
A fair job. That's all.
It will last, I said. He agreed.
And walked into the marketplace in silence.
Calmness everywhere in this world.
It was then I walked farther until
My feet ached terribly in the bleak
Predawn movements of fog, covering
Divine inquiry; those blankets upon my feet
Upon my feet.

Selah

## III. Remembrance

The serene did glean with a slumberous sheen
On the ripples that gently tossed;
A spine sat in recline
With droplets forcing themselves on my shape like dogma.
No. No. I do not want that pain anymore, anymore
From the likes of Ilsadore[3]
Rising like a billowing mud packet, sublime in form.
But why said I to the corrugated sky in the midst of woe...
It is too frivolous...these lines, they do not blend
As they should: they clash between love and eight o'clock.
Le seul bien qui me reste au monde, wrote de Musset...[4]
The eyes dive beneath the dying waters, cool...
His being was stung to the bottom of second self's rung

---

3 Refers to variant spelling of Iseulte in story of Tristan and Iseulte.

4 Alfred de Musset: French poet and writer. In his poem titled "Tristesse": the concluding lines "le seul bien qui me reste au monde est d'avoir quelquefois pleuré" mean "the only good that remains to me in this world is to weep sometimes."

In the moribund passion.
How that vinegar hurt he said to me in the abundant
Patience of a Job. If London bridge should ever
Fall, it could not restore Ilsadore.
Those tears tears tears fell with the years years years…
On a trodden shore below with imprints on the sand.
Listen! Mark me! I give you hope…hope for another round
Until there was no sound sound sound of
Any other round round round.
Tis not in the deck the ace is lost for mortal sight and
Spirit sound.
Is this Paris? Where is the gay
That should spray away the day? It is gone
From this memory.
Come, let's to Toulouse and let us see
The ugly sadness of memory in time.

I, I really must go out to the birds in the snow
In Bretagne…the only recollection my friend,
Est d'avoir quelquefois pleuré.
Wait. You don't see the advantages of this painting.
I still do not want it I tell you no and no again!
This folly is not what I want!
To tell you the hot, licking peremptory evanescent truth?
Nay, my lines are a shell of sorrow
To give the world its bliss…
In nadir time…….
Perchance.
Surely you shall try another round to try out the sound.
This is more in heaven than meets the sight of your
Haggard mouth and plaintive cry…
In the quest for what is why.
I am spent…through in moribund passion
Let it buried be…in the sea in the sea
Drinking and drinking more ice tea.
My vices were my virtues so call me a
Parisien heathen. It's all up there

In the godly infinite air…
More love in this world than that.

I must give thought to this in Munich.
We shall see, watch the wave gently break upon him broken.
I know, I know
There is no happiness to grow
In the wild adulterous tules by the shore anymore.
I said I do thrice and felt the rice…
And kissed hot lips arched high
And heard the heartening tenderness of a baby cry…

But all is spent now.
You do wonder why love has never made you cry.
My friend, to be born is to cry and die.
You callow cheek! Away with your persevering insolence!
Let me die in the quest for why.
Now I must away for Berlin and ask again
For the givingness of an endlessness.
The days end and beg for sleep
In one-eyed merriness in sleepiness,
After that cry in the mucous sunset
Of the elm-shading leaf…
Denying a grief to make another round.
Selah

## IV. A Time for Beer

Drinking. Call it passion in motion terms, he said.
All grizzled in the city lights warming nights…
Yes, I find the heart quite beauteous…
But you say for a woman?
Ah, listening my friend this is not tale, a truism if any…
I married for the stuff that obsesses the stoutest
Of hearts, and you?
This the time for drink at its damndest, you think so?
Pardon me, is this Jack's turn of the screw? Of course,
Dearie what do you think? Ve want more dis stuff…
Does the tuba and drum music play loud enough? Nein.
She doesn't lay enough…Louder please!
Don't…don't that hurts me there. Away.

Take that picture away! Off me you young wench!
I don't care. I don't care how long is your hair.
I've had my fun and lusty desire with the false faces
And de beer and de vimen…
Vat? You don't believe me?
Your turn with Ilsadore…
I've had enough of her…she tickles.
Dis voman too big. Pour me another.
And here, here for this artist?
Is this Ilium? Hell no it ain't. You from the states?
Glad to meet you and your face. Wait.
I saw you in London two months before
When the fog rolled in over my shoes and
Kept the cramps away without the slippers.
Let him try to sell this painting of Venus. You cannot.
I want no part of such a deal; this whole idea
Is senseless, useless, nonsense.
The city lights on foggy nights keep them warm
In the story of a night time glory
In the dusky air and blown far away to never and a day.
Crossing in tiptoes on an endless stare in Flanders field
Where hearts lay forever and ten months to the time,
Of another surrender when they shall be thrown into
The air and die in dust.
Time is life and care murders. How do you know?
Here drink this and melt away the care of the hellish day
In May. I don't care what you're selling; I have enough
Paints to hold my memory for a lifetime, don't you see?
Love's a fairy tale played on the harps of fools.
        The pains pains pains
        Of life's scarlet rains
        Scarlet rains.

Selah

## V. Lad

Would you care to buy this painting?
Monsieur? Take it; monsieur…
I am too young for this,

But you'll grow into it…I'm sure
In time you will.
Non! Monsieur…je ne peux pas…take it monsieur
What is wrong with you people…do not want ecstasy?
This light eternal to keep cities warm?
This cannot be but folly: birth and death
On the slippery gradations of Fate…
Back to the sea into your shell…the seasons shall
Warm you and tis to Cyprus we go…
Those beings do not wish you in their eyes anymore
You cannot bridge the cliffs of hope…too high for
I, I am a child monsieur. This I cannot take from you.
This morning sunset in my father's death;
No time for paintings that burn color into my cheek
Shall not help your cause any, monsieur I
Must sell more apples to pay off the death, my own?
Please lad, I'll sell it cheap, an only hope…
Non monsieur, I cannot take it for my soul's sake
In this time of all times, a time of grief, I cannot;
I cannot at any time at all;
It is the folly of my father to believe in such…
It is the folly of my brother to believe in such as much
It is Sunday…I must hurry to church and pray
For money to carry me over the churchyard…
Death is the expense of mortality…
It is expensive you know.
Such a lovely face, is it Venus?
Ah, yes how did you know? Oh I know…
Love's immortality; you are missing divinity…
More divine that all the gods of yesteryear
Of all days in the mouth of eternity atop
The jaws of the earth.
Forgive me monsieur, I must away
To the churchyard…
Let the poor boy go, he does not know
What tis to fight and stay alone nights
Heaving your beauty above a weary head
On top my bed linens all blue and white…
To match the scarless face of night

The scarless face of night...
All in one goodnight to ladies...

Selah

## VI. A Last Song of Wine

I shall walk in the snow...out where the birds they sing
And smooth their feathers on a wing...
Please, sir, this picture I presume.
Dare not presume, my son, the mind is an axis of presumption
And glory. Tis color enough...greens, blues...and that face
Take it away...no...bring it back
I like those strokes pinned in black...
Let us drink the world of grief and bid happy days return.
I love love now...
A time to go
A time to go
To where I don't know...
Most to a grave, sir. Love kills the best of men.
Mortals feel, I tell you...
Mortals feel.
The last cup of wine
Shall waste away the time and the wine
Of life tossed to the yellow and sunburnt winds that cake
With age's wrinkles and old defeats.
This painting, do you like it?
That is what I want...she is so pretty, a beauty...
How frail is man in the world
Pasting vanity on a sign and pointing to it in time!
As the ravages drain my face,
I lose my place.
Among you mortals...
And blood perishes for ideals and fools live to tell it.
Beauty is love and love is the world's song:
And grief laments over a still pool
Sending tears in rings of agony...
Ah, that the world were my canvas!

Love would live live live
To give and give and give.

Is it sin? Is it sin? To live and die to put it in?
Your heart to die and those left in cold mystery behind
Call tragedy farce and farce idiotic delight?
For life as a mist should only be kissed in a mist
Of rapturous moment…a lit candle to flicker.
Helas, qu'avec facilité on se laisse persuader par
Les personnes qu'on l'aime.[5]
Gouton voir si le vin nest bon[6]…Wine is the best life…
In the season vintage…drink and sing for the dead morning.
I haven't long…I haven't long
Life is short and death is long.
This will comfort my throat! Drink!
And easy goes away the pain of grief. But
I approve, I approve of that portrait…
The dying want love most.
Only words have the pomp to boast;
Give me toast, a toast, a last breath
And drown the waves of eternal death;
Breathe while you can you mortals be
And drink your wine most merrily!
The saddest songs are never was or could be…
That's called tragedy.

Selah

## VII. Genesis

I hear the cries, said I
With the red sky above me.
Give it milk
And kindness
And virtue

---

5 In English: "Alas, with what ease it is to be persuaded by the one who one loves."

6 French drinking song: "Taste to see if the wine is good…"

And patience...
Need will proclaim it, you parents!

And of all things it shall inherit
The legacy of life;
O teach it to give with flooded eyes...
Tears of love and sympathy.
This babe likes this painting!
More, more of these
Should play in the future's leaves
That spray in the ocean breeze
And gird their souls with promise amid misfortune.
And when he is growing let all the heavens
Shower the hot most earth
With revelations that sting the heart
Into believing...
Love is God and God is love...
Sing it to the end of your eschatology...
If mercy will not.

Selah

## VII. Exodus

And when bleeding
Shall drape the heart
In sadness among your days
Pick the grape and listen for the birds
In the fleecy snow;
They come and go...come and go
Today a thousand tomorrows ago.
Lovers, love with the blood
And soul...
And spirit for when you do
You shall conquer...
And we shall be human:
Mortals feel, I tell you
Mortals feel,
Mortals.
Ah, Venus what labor is it to understanding!

O human heart, forgive…
For beauty is love and love is beauty
To the vanishing dreams of lads…
To the notes of angelic beauty…
The stuff withal of love again a thousand times…
Are blessed in the season vintage
Of eternal hope to shine.

I sing the world's song of love…
For all to hear with the heart…
With love and hope and vigilance.

Selah

## Perpetual Snow

Calculated
by a mathematical priest,
smart geometries
hang hidden
as the canary
yellow sun
blankets the city.

As sky gathers
in our windows,
we note
the vapor trail
of a jet overhead.

Despite the sun's oomph,
we remark
the perpetual snow
that never melts
on our mountain tops
high above our field
that includes cacti,
thistles, loofah,
and other fruit
that ripen inwards.

While we drink summer
from the sun's bread,
we sense
the mating ecstasy
of the cosmic dance
by the pulse of time.

We soon realize that
despite the murk
of a summer seabed,
the advent
of grace
happens
as June's lightning
batters the coast.

## Lovers Bloom

In the breezes willow boughs sway
as cows graze in the sunned
age spots and bushy brows
of this brother of the hinterland
as he and his love
venture to the coast.

As God is my witness,
they know lovers bloom
in each other all along;
they live a poem of ecstasy
and a storm of unblinking truth
amid seagulls of longing.

They play, hug,
and reach
through braking sea foam
amid dove-gray pelicans
and sea-worshipping geese.

As wings of night fall,
a choir of heavenly galaxies
occurs amid
a passionate adoration
of this particular earth.

Soon one enjoys
midnight-kissed nightingales
as night winds into morning
as they await
the eyelashes of dawn.

Such is God's merciful
generosity
to invite them to behold
the divine light.

## Solitary Man

In a season of wild love
next to a wind-swept sea

a solitary man who walks
with Andromeda and Capricorn

whose soul
is no stranger to earth,

turns away from the lairs of lying and
those wastelands of mistaken hunts

and continues to where orchards
of the resurrected meet, and finds

his heart now overflows
with sunrise.

19616046R00048

Made in the USA
Lexington, KY
28 November 2018